Jennifer Lopez

ABDO
Publishing Company

Big
Buddy BOOKS
Buddy Bios

by Sarah Tieck

VISIT US AT
www.abdopublishing.com

Published by ABDO Publishing Company, PO Box 398166, Minneapolis, MN 55439.

Copyright © 2012 by Abdo Consulting Group, Inc. International copyrights reserved in all countries. No part of this book may be reproduced in any form without written permission from the publisher. Big Buddy Books™ is a trademark and logo of ABDO Publishing Company.

Printed in the United States of America, North Mankato, Minnesota.
102011
012012

 PRINTED ON RECYCLED PAPER

Coordinating Series Editor: Rochelle Baltzer
Contributing Editors: Megan M. Gunderson, BreAnn Rumsch, Marcia Zappa
Graphic Design: Maria Hosley
Cover Photograph: *AP Photo*: Rex Features via AP Images.
Interior Photographs/Illustrations: *AP Photo*: Alex J. Berliner/abimages via AP Images (p. 27), Jill Connelly
    (p. 22), Paul Drinkwater/NBC/NBCU Photo Bank via AP Images (p. 23), Krista Kennell/Sipa Press/
    jlopezwangotangokk.050/1105151751 (Sipa via AP Images) (p. 29), Peter Kramer/NBC/NBC NewsWire via AP
    Images (p. 11), Mark Lennihan (p. 19), Frank Micelotta/Fox/PictureGroup via AP Images (p. 25), Neil Munns
    (p. 13), Norman Ng/NBCU Photo Bank via AP Images (p. 20), Suzanne Plunkett (p. 9), Mark J. Terrill
    (p. 17); *Getty Images*: Getty Images (p. 15), Ke.Mazur (p. 7), Kmazur (p. 7), Albert L. Ortega/WireImage (p. 15),
    Sgranitz/WireImage (p. 21), Jim Smeal/WireImage (p. 11), Noel Vasquez (p. 5); *Shutterstock*: Artifan (p. 9).

Library of Congress Cataloging-in-Publication Data

Tieck, Sarah, 1976-
  Jennifer Lopez : famous entertainer / Sarah Tieck.
    p. cm. -- (Big buddy biographies)
  ISBN 978-1-61783-225-3
  1. Lopez, Jennifer, 1970---Juvenile literature. 2. Actors--United States--Biography--Juvenile literature. 3. Singers-
-United States--Biography--Juvenile literature. 4. Hispanic American actors--Biography--Juvenile literature. 5.
Hispanic American singers--Biography--Juvenile literature. I. Title.
  PN2287.L634T54 2012
  791.4302'8092--dc23
  [B]
                              2011037821

Contents

Jennifer has appeared on *American Idol* as a judge.

Triple-Threat Star

Jennifer Lopez is a talented dancer, singer, and actress. People who can do all three are called "triple threats." Fans around the world love Jennifer's work!

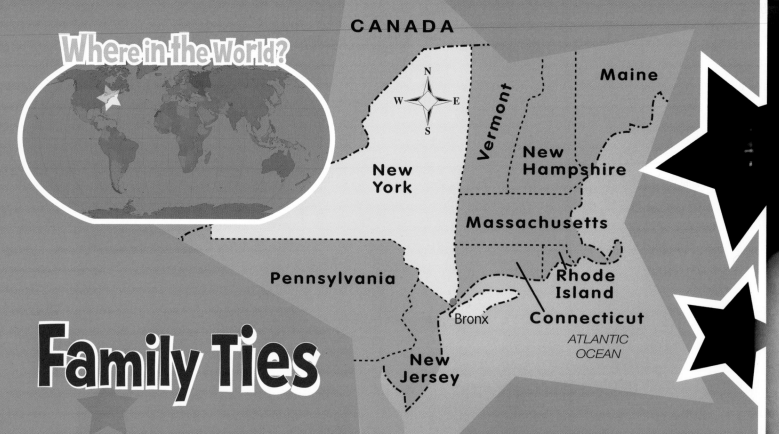

Where in the World?

CANADA

Maine

Vermont

New Hampshire

New York

Massachusetts

Pennsylvania

Rhode Island

Connecticut

Bronx

ATLANTIC OCEAN

New Jersey

Family Ties

Jennifer Lynn Lopez was born in the Bronx, New York, on July 24, 1969. Her parents are David and Guadalupe Lopez. Jennifer has an older sister named Leslie and a younger sister named Lynda.

Jennifer's parents taught her to work hard. This helped her to be a good student. She spent her free time listening to music and watching movies with her family.

Jennifer and her parents are close.
Her dad (*left*) worked with computers.
Her mom (*right*) was a teacher.

A Proud Family

People from Latin America are called Latinos. People in the United States whose families are from there are also called Latinos.

Jennifer's parents were both born in Ponce, Puerto Rico. As a Latino, Jennifer is proud of her family's **culture**. Latin culture is known for its food and music.

In 1999, Jennifer was the grand marshal of New York City's Puerto Rican Day Parade. This was a special honor.

San Juan (*right*) is the largest city in Puerto Rico. Ponce is the third-largest city.

Did you know...
In high school, Jennifer enjoyed track, tennis, and other sports.

Starting Out

Growing up, Jennifer and her sisters enjoyed music. They sang and danced for fun whenever they could! Jennifer took singing and dancing lessons. She hoped to work as a **performer** one day.

After high school, Jennifer worked at a law office. But, she continued dancing and performing. In 1990, Jennifer got a job on a popular television show called *In Living Color*. She was one of the show's dancers.

On *In Living Color*, Jennifer was part of the show's dance group called the Fly Girls.

Jennifer worked with Jim Carrey on *In Living Color*. Jim went on to become a famous actor.

13

Where in the World?

Jennifer moved to Los Angeles, California, to be closer to her work. She left her friends and family behind. At first, she was very homesick.

Soon, Jennifer got more acting and dancing work. She acted in television shows and movies. She also became a backup dancer for famous singer Janet Jackson. Jennifer even danced in one of Janet's music videos!

Janet Jackson is known for her singing and dancing talent. Jennifer learned much about the music business while working with Janet.

Jennifer (*right*) changed her appearance to look like Selena in the movie.

Big Break

In 1997, Jennifer starred in *Selena*. This movie is about famous Latino singer Selena Quintanilla Pérez. Jennifer sang, danced, and acted in it. People noticed how talented she was!

The movie was a hit. And, it proved to be an important **role** for Jennifer. She was proud of her work.

Jennifer attended the *Selena* premiere. She was excited to see her work in public!

Growing Talent

After *Selena*, Jennifer got more movie **roles**. In 1997, she was in *U Turn* with well-known actors. The next year, she had a voice part in the cartoon movie *Antz*.

Each role improved Jennifer's skills. Soon, she was one of Hollywood's most popular actresses! She also became the highest-paid Latino actress.

Jennifer was named as a possible winner of a Golden Globe award for her work on *Selena*. These awards are given each year to honor accomplishments in television and film.

Crossing Over

Jennifer loved working as an actress. But, she also dreamed of becoming a singer. So, she worked hard making music. In 1999, she **released** her first album. It is called *On the 6*.

The album was a hit! Some popular songs were "If You Had My Love" and "Let's Get Loud." They mixed Latin music with dance music and **rhythm and blues**.

In 1999, Jennifer performed at the VH1 Vogue Fashion Awards.

19

Double the Fun

Jennifer's acting and singing success continued. In 2001, she starred in *The Wedding Planner* and **released** her second album, *J.Lo*. Both the movie and the album were very popular!

In 2002, Jennifer starred in *Maid in Manhattan*. Also that year, she released the album *This is Me...Then*. She released *Rebirth* in 2005 and *Brave* in 2007.

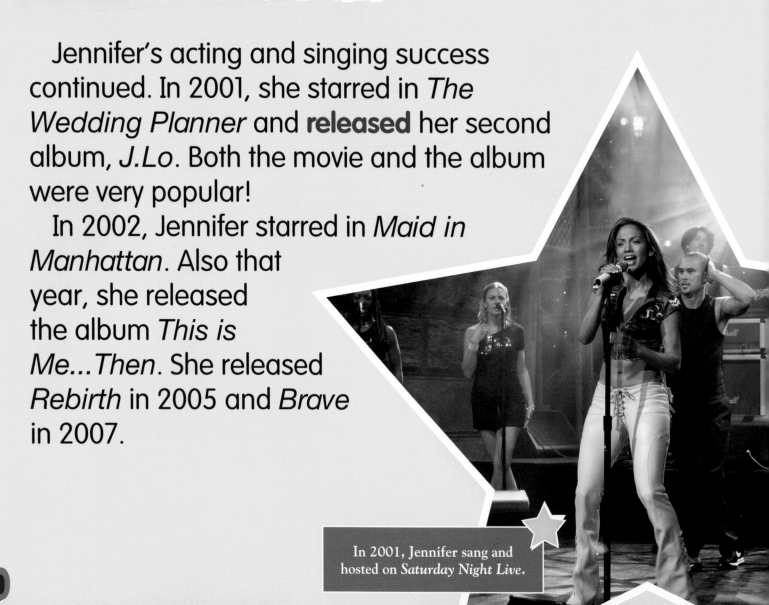

In 2001, Jennifer sang and hosted on *Saturday Night Live.*

Matthew McConaughey starred with
Jennifer in *The Wedding Planner*.

21

Working Life

Jennifer works hard to sing, dance, and act well. For her music, she spends many hours practicing before **performing**. She performs live concerts around the world.

Jennifer travels for her acting work, too. She may spend days or months on location filming a movie. Jennifer also attends events and meets fans. Her fans are always excited to see her!

Jennifer is a businesswoman. She has clothing (*left*) and perfume lines.

Jennifer has appeared on popular television shows, including *The Tonight Show with Jay Leno.*

American Idol

In 2010, Jennifer got a new opportunity. She was asked to be a judge on the tenth season of *American Idol*.

This popular television show finds talented singers. Each season begins with tryouts. Jennifer helps choose a small group of finalists to **perform**. They **compete** to be named the next American Idol.

On *American Idol*, famous singer Steven Tyler (*left*) and Jennifer joined Randy Jackson (*second from right*) and Ryan Seacrest (*right*). Scotty McCreery (*center*) was the season 10 winner.

Off the Stage

When she's not working, Jennifer enjoys spending time with her family. She has twins named Max and Emme. Their father is famous singer Marc Anthony.

Jennifer is also active in the community. She attends Latino events. And, she likes to help people and **charities**.

Emme and Max Anthony were born in February 2008. They sometimes attend events with their mom.

27

Buzz

Jennifer's opportunities continue to grow. In 2010, she starred in the movie *The Back-up Plan*. And in 2011, she **released** an album called *Love?*

In 2012, Jennifer returned to *American Idol*. She also acted in the movie *What to Expect When You're Expecting*. Fans are excited to see what's next for Jennifer Lopez!

One popular song from *Love?* is "On the Floor." Famous rapper Pitbull (*right*) raps in this song.

Snapshot

⭐ **Name**: Jennifer Lynn Lopez

⭐ **Birthday**: July 24, 1969

⭐ **Birthplace**: Bronx, New York

⭐ **Albums**: *On the 6, J.Lo, This Is Me...Then, Rebirth, Brave, Love?*

⭐ **Appearances**: *In Living Color, Selena, U Turn, Antz, The Wedding Planner, Maid in Manhattan, The Back-up Plan, American Idol, What to Expect When You're Expecting*

Important Words

charity a group or a fund that helps people in need.

compete to take part in a contest between two or more persons or groups.

culture (KUHL-chuhr) the arts, beliefs, and ways of life of a group of people.

perform to do something in front of an audience.

release to make available to the public.

rhythm (RIH-thuhm) **and blues** a form of popular music that features a strong beat. It is inspired by jazz, gospel, and blues styles.

role a part an actor plays.

Web Sites

To learn more about Jennifer Lopez, visit ABDO Publishing Company online. Web sites about Jennifer Lopez are featured on our Book Links page. These links are routinely monitored and updated to provide the most current information available.

www.abdopublishing.com

Index